Introducing Continents

North America

Chris Oxlade

Raintree

Raintree is an imprint of Capstone Global Library Limited, a company incorporated in England and Wales having its registered office at 7 Pilgrim Street, London, EC4V 6LB – Registered company number: 6695582

www.raintreepublishers.co.uk
myorders@raintreepublishers.co.uk

Text © Capstone Global Library Limited 2014
First published in hardback in 2014
Paperback edition first published in 2015
The moral rights of the proprietor have been asserted.

Edited by Dan Nunn, Rebecca Rissman, Sian Smith, and Helen Cox Cannons
Designed by Philippa Jenkins
Original illustrations © Capstone Global Library Ltd 2014
Picture research by Liz Alexander and Tristan Leverett
Production by Vicki Fitzgerald
Originated by Capstone Global Library Ltd
Printed and bound in China by Leo Paper Products Ltd

ISBN 978 1 406 26298 8 (hardback)
17 16 15 14 13
10 9 8 7 6 5 4 3 2 1

ISBN 978 1 406 26307 7 (paperback)
18 17 16 15 14
10 9 8 7 6 5 4 3 2 1

British Library Cataloguing in Publication Data
Oxlade, Chris
Introducing North America. – (Introducing continents)
A full catalogue record for this book is available from the British Library.

Acknowledgements
We would like to thank the following for permission to reproduce photographs: Getty Images pp. 11 (Rick Gerharter/Lonely Planet Images), 13 (Robyn Beck/AFP), 17 (Ingram Publishing), 18 (Wayne R Bilenduke/Stone), 19 (John A. Rizzo/Stockbyte), 21 (Tim Graham), 26 (Susana Gonzalez/Bloomberg), 27 (Stephen Brashear); Shutterstock pp. 6 (© Bryan Busovicki), 8 (© Gail Johnson), 9 (© kavram), 15 (© markrhiggins), 16 (© Anton Foltin), 20 (© aceshot1), 23 (© Kamira), 24 (© S.Borisov); Science Photo Library p. 14 (Jeffrey Lepore); SuperStock pp. 7 (age footstock), 10 (Design Pics), 12 (Jeff Schultz/Alaska Stock), 25 (Susan E. Pease/age footstock).

Cover photographs of Horseshoe Bend, Grand Canyon and a shaded relief map of North America reproduced with permission of Shutterstock (© somchaij, © AridOcean); image of cowboys riding the range in Montana, USA reproduced with permission of SuperStock (© age fotostock).

Every effort has been made to contact copyright holders of material reproduced in this book. Any omissions will be rectified in subsequent printings if notice is given to the publisher.

Disclaimer
All the internet addresses (URLs) given in this book were valid at the time of going to press. However, due to the dynamic nature of the internet, some addresses may have changed, or sites may have changed or ceased to exist since publication. While the author and publisher regret any inconvenience this may cause readers, no responsibility for any such changes can be accepted by either the author or the publisher.

Contents

Some words are shown in bold, **like this**. You can find out what they mean by looking in the glossary.

About North America

North America is one of the world's seven **continents**. A continent is a huge area of land. North America is the third largest continent. It stretches almost from the **equator** in the south to the **Arctic** in the north.

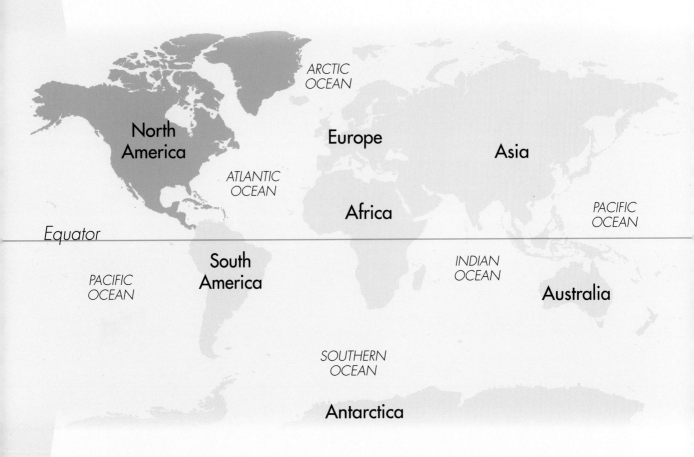

ARCTIC OCEAN

North America

Europe

Asia

ATLANTIC OCEAN

Africa

PACIFIC OCEAN

Equator

PACIFIC OCEAN

South America

INDIAN OCEAN

Australia

SOUTHERN OCEAN

Antarctica

North America sits between the Atlantic Ocean in the east and the Pacific Ocean in the west. North America is connected to the continent of South America by a narrow strip of land. This area is called Central America.

North America fact file	
Area	24,490,000 square kilometres (9,456,000 square miles)
Population	542 million
Number of countries	23
Highest mountain	Mount McKinley at 6,194 metres (20,322 feet)
Longest river	Missouri at 3,768 kilometres (2,341 miles)

Famous places

There are many amazing natural landmarks in North America. The Grand Canyon in Arizona, USA, is 445 kilometres (277 miles) long. Niagara Falls and Yellowstone National Park also are popular places to visit.

In some places, the Grand Canyon is 1.6 kilometres (one mile) deep.

This is the pyramid of the Niches in the ancient city of El Tajin in Mexico.

There are many famous buildings, too. In Mexico, there are pyramids built about 500 years ago by people called the Aztecs. Modern buildings include the CN Tower in Toronto, Canada, and the Hoover Dam in the United States.

Geography

The largest **mountain range** in North America is the Rocky Mountains, in the west. The Rockies stretch nearly 5,000 kilometres (3,100 miles) from Mexico to Alaska. The Appalachian Mountains are on the east side of North America.

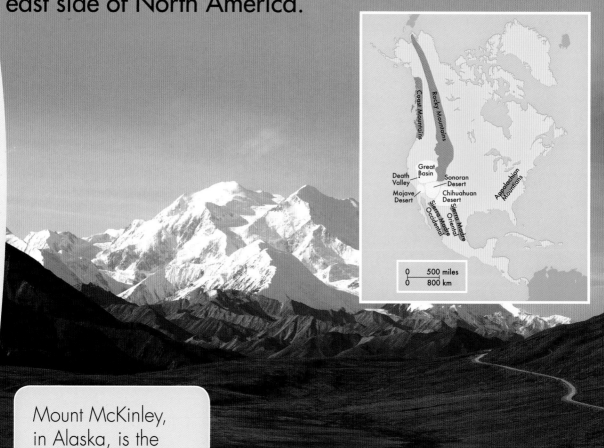

Mount McKinley, in Alaska, is the highest mountain in North America.

This part of the Mojave Desert is called Death Valley because it is so hot and dry.

There are **deserts** in the southwest of North America. They include the Mojave Desert in California and the Sonoran Desert in New Mexico. The Great **Plains** is a huge area of flat land in the centre of North America. It is also called the **prairie**.

There are five huge lakes along the border between the United States and Canada. They are called the Great Lakes. Lake Superior is one of the Great Lakes. It is the world's largest **freshwater** lake.

This photograph shows Lake Superior in winter.

Yukon River

Mackenzie River

Columbia River

Lake Superior St. Lawrence River

Mississippi River

Missouri River

Ohio River

Colorado River

Rio Grande

Hudson River

The Great Lakes

0   500 miles
0   800 km

This paddle steamer is taking tourists on a trip along the Mississippi.

The Missouri is the longest river in North America. It is 3,768 kilometres (2,341 miles) long. It flows across the centre of the United States and into the Mississippi River. The St Lawrence River connects the Great Lakes with the Atlantic Ocean.

Weather

North America has many different types of weather. In the south, it is tropical. This means it is hot and there is lots of rain. In the north, it is very cold all year round, and there is lots of snow.

In the far north of North America, there are times during the winter when it stays dark all day.

Hurricane Rita caused this flooding in the state of Louisiana in the United States.

Extreme weather sometimes strikes North America. **Hurricanes** are giant storms. They bring powerful winds and heavy rains to Central America, the Caribbean, and the southeast of the United States. **Tornadoes** also hit the United States.

Animals

An amazing variety of animals live in North America. Polar bears live in the far north, and grizzly bears live in the forests and mountains further south. Bison live on the **plains**. They are also known as buffalo.

This grizzly bear is living high in the Rocky Mountains.

Alligators live in swamps called the Everglades in the USA.

Alligators live in lakes, rivers, and **swamps** in the southeast of the United States. Hundreds of different types of birds make their homes in the rainforests of Central America. Jaguars live in the rainforests, too.

Plants

A giant plant grows in the **deserts** in the south of North America. It is the saguaro cactus. It grows up to 15 metres (49 feet) high. It survives on very little water.

These saguaro cacti are growing in the desert in Arizona, USA.

These enormous trees are giant redwoods.

There are vast conifer forests in the north of North America. Conifer trees stay green all year round. Giant redwood trees grow here, too. They are the tallest trees in the world. They grow up to 112 metres (367 feet) high.

People

American Indians were the first people to live in North America. There are many groups of American Indians all over North America. People from all over Europe settled in North America too, including from Britain, France, and Spain.

Inuit people live in the far north of North America.

People from many different groups live in New York City.

Most people in the United States speak English. Many people in Central America and Mexico speak Spanish, and many people in Canada speak French. American Indians often speak their own languages.

Sport and culture

Baseball, basketball, and ice hockey are popular sports in the United States and Canada. American football began in the United States. The Super Bowl is the biggest game of the year.

This crowd are enjoying a game of baseball at the Cincinnati Reds.

This reggae band is playing on the island of Jamaica.

Hollywood is in Los Angeles, California. It is the centre of the film industry in the United States. Hundreds of films are made here every year. Popular music in North America includes country music in the United States and reggae music in the islands of the Caribbean.

Countries

There are 23 countries in North America. The **continent** is made up mostly of three very large countries. These are the United States of America (the USA), Canada, and Mexico. Canada is the second largest country in the world, after Russia.

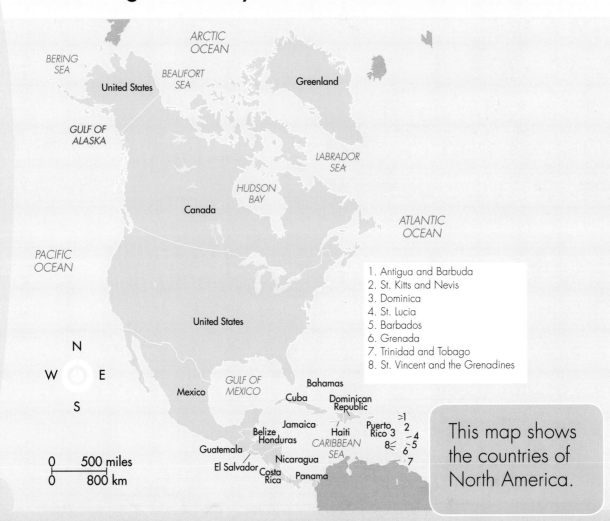

1. Antigua and Barbuda
2. St. Kitts and Nevis
3. Dominica
4. St. Lucia
5. Barbados
6. Grenada
7. Trinidad and Tobago
8. St. Vincent and the Grenadines

This map shows the countries of North America.

This is a street in Havana, the capital city of Cuba.

Most of the countries of North America are islands in the Caribbean Sea, such as Cuba and Jamaica. Greenland is the world's largest island, but it is not a country. It is part of Denmark, a country in Europe.

23

Cities and countryside

New York City, Los Angeles, Mexico City, and Toronto are some of the cities in North America with the greatest number of people. Mexico City is the largest city in North America. Around 20 million people live there. New York is an important world business centre.

There are dozens of skyscrapers in the centre of New York City.

This is the main street in April, a town in Massachusetts, USA.

There are thousands of small towns in the **plains** of North America. Many people who live here are farmers who grow wheat and raise cattle. In Central America, most people work on small farms. They grow coffee, sugar, or bananas.

Natural resources and products

Trees are cut down in the forests of Canada and the United States. The wood goes to make furniture, houses, and many other wooden objects. Oil and gas are found under the ground and sea in many places.

This oil rig is in the Gulf of Mexico.

Boeing aeroplanes are made in this giant factory.

North America has many different industries. Cars are made in the United States, Canada, and Mexico. Boeing aeroplanes are made near Seattle, USA. Silicon Valley in California is the home of the US computer industry.

Fun facts

- The Panama Canal cuts through the middle of the country of Panama. It carries huge ships between the Atlantic Ocean and the Pacific Ocean.

- Tornado Alley is an area in the centre of the United States where many **tornadoes** hit every year.

- Greenland is covered with a sheet of ice that is more than 3 kilometres (nearly 2 miles) thick in some places.

- The Boeing aircraft factory near Seattle, USA, is the world's largest building.

Quiz

1. Which part of North America is the biggest island in the world?

2. What is the largest mountain range in North America?

3. Who built pyramids in Mexico?

4. What is the world's largest freshwater lake?

4. Lake Superior

3. The Aztecs

2. The Rocky Mountains in the United States

1. Greenland

Glossary

Arctic area of Earth around the North Pole, where it is always cold

continent one of seven huge areas of land on Earth

desert area of land that gets very little rain

equator imaginary line running around the middle of Earth

freshwater water that fills rivers and lakes. It is not salty like seawater.

hurricane fierce storm that brings strong winds and heavy rain

mountain range long line of mountains

plains flat lands

prairie huge area of grassland or farmland

swamps places where the ground is muddy or flooded

tornado spinning column of air that brings very strong winds

Find out more

Books

Horrible Geography of the World, Anita Ganeri (Scholastic, 2010)

North America (Exploring Continents), Tristan Boyer Binns (Heinemann Library, 2008)

Oxford First Atlas (OUP, 2010)

Websites to visit

kids.discovery.com/tell-me/people-and-places/ our-7-continents
Games, puzzles, and activities about the seven continents can be found on this website.

kids.nationalgeographic.com/kids/games/ geographygames/copycat
This fun game helps you to find the continents on a map of the world.

www.worldatlas.com
This site has lots of maps, facts, and figures about continents.

Index